The Journey to Self-Love

Michael Mosesian

The Journey to Self-Love
Copyright © 2023 by Dr. Michael Mosesian
All rights reserved.

No part of this book may be reproduced or used in any manner whatsoever without the express written permission of the Author. This includes photocopying, recording, or by any information storage and retrieval system, without permission in writing from the author. Neither the author nor the publisher makes any claims to the outcome by the readers. This book is intended as educational purposes only and does not replace or supplant professional guidance from medical practitioners.

Publisher: Absolute Author Publishing House

Library of Congress In-Publication Data
Mosesian, Michael

ISBN: 978-1-64953-842-0

Table of Contents

Author's Note 1
Chapter 1: Daily Life 3
   Stop Waiting for the Right Time 5
   The Friday Feeling 7
   The Joy of the Simple Things 8
   Taking on the Day 10
   The Work-Life Balance 12
   Monday Motivation 13
Chapter 2: The Journey of Life 15
   Birth and Childhood 17
   Coming of Age 18
   Falling in Love 20
   Getting Married 22
   Blessings Unfold 23
Chapter 3: The Power of Love 25
   The First Meeting 27
   The Promise of a Lifetime 29
   The Gift of Partnership 31
   The Beauty of Relationships 33
   The Power of Love 35
Chapter 4: The Aging Journey 37
   The Golden Years 39
   The Art of Growing Older 41
   Reflections on Time 43
   The Wisdom of Age 45
   Embracing the Journey 47
Chapter 5: Breaking Free from Stereotypes 49
   Unique Reflections 51
   Unchained Beauty 53
   Individuality 55
   The Power of Social Influence 57
   Breaking Free 59
   Discovering Self 61

Chapter 6: Discovering Your True Self **63**
   The Path to Self-Discovery..65
   Self-Expression..67
   The Freedom to Be Yourself..69
   Self-Realization 71
   The Promise of Personal Growth 73

Chapter 7: Loving Yourself **75**
   The Beauty of Self-Love..77
   The Power of Self-Worth 79
   The Strength of Self-Confidence..................................81
   The Freedom of Self-Forgiveness.................................83
   The Miracle of Self-Acceptance...................................86

Chapter 8: Finding Purpose and Meaning **89**
   New Dawns and Fresh Starts......................................91
   The Journey Through Life..93
   The Meaning of Life 94
   The Journey to Fulfilment 96
   The Gifts of Life Unseen 98

Chapter 9: Overcoming Adversity **101**
   Rise Again...103
   Embracing Change 104
   Turning Setbacks into Comebacks.............................106
   Learning from Mistakes 107
   The Journey of Life..109
   Sculpting Success in the Sands of Struggle................111
   Painting Futures on the Canvas of Time 113
   The right time is now 115

Chapter 10: Overcoming Fears and Anxieties................ **117**
   An Unwelcome Guest...119
   Facing Your Fears..120
   The Courage to Be Yourself......................................122
   The Fear of Rejection 123

Chapter 11: The Importance of Family 125
    The Love of a Parent 127
    The Support of a Sibling.........................128
    The Guidance of a Grandparent 129
    The Joy of a Child 130
    The Strength of a Family 131

Chapter 12: Healing 133
    The Scar of Healing.............................135
    Healing from Loss 136
    Broken Heart 137
    The Sun Has Left Me 138
    The Loss of Love 140

Chapter 13: Finding Your Own Path 141
    The Search for Purpose..........................143
    The Quest for Happiness 145
    The Journey of Self-Discovery...................146
    The Gift of Hope................................147
    Love, the River of Life...........................148

Chapter 14: The Resilience of the Human Heart. 149
    The Ability to Forgive...........................151
    The Capacity to Love 152
    The Strength to Endure 153
    The Faith to Believe in Yourself..................154
    Tomorrow's Promise.............................155
    Seize the Day....................................156

Acknowledgments: 157

Author's Note

Welcome to "The Journey to Self-Love", a book filled with touching poems that encourage us to love ourselves a little more each day.

Every poem in this book is a small light, guiding us through the different paths we walk in life. From the tough times that shape us to the happy moments that lift us up, these poems capture the heart of our shared human experience.

In this book, you'll find poems about happiness, personal growth, resilience and the importance of loving yourself.

Whether you're going through a hard time or enjoying a peaceful moment, these poems are here to bring hope, inspiration, and comfort. They remind us of our own strength and value, and the beauty found in every step of our path.

Join this conversation through poetry. Let these verses talk to you, reflect your emotions, and light your way. As you read, you might find these poems not only as words on a page, but as a reflection of your own journey to self-love.

Get ready to see yourself in a new light with "The Journey to Self-Love". Uncover life's lessons, one poem at a time.

Chapter 1:

Daily Life

CHAPTER I: DAILY LIFE

Stop Waiting for the Right Time

I wake each morning,
With a dream in my heart.
I know what I must do,
But I'm afraid to start.

I tell myself, "Tomorrow,"
But tomorrow never comes.
The days turn into weeks,
And the weeks into months.

The elusive "right time" remains out of reach,
The right time will never come.
If I want to achieve my dreams,
I must take action today.

So I close my eyes,
And take a deep breath.
I know that I'm scared,
But I'm also excited.

Today, I'll take the first stride,
Towards success, I won't hide.
Fear won't hinder my chosen quest,
The time is now, for dreams to come true.

So, why wait any longer?
Don't wait for the perfect sign.
Now is the moment, the time to begin.
Start today, make your dreams align.

The Friday Feeling

The Friday feeling,
When the week is through,
And all that's left is
The weekend brew.

The feeling of relief,
The feeling of joy,
The feeling of freedom,
To do as I please, enjoy.

I'm going to enjoy myself,
And not think about tomorrow,
Living in the present,
And let the good times flow.

So here's to Friday, and the weekend,
And all the fun that's to be had,
I'll seize every moment,
And not let anything get me down.

The Joy of the Simple Things

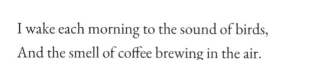

I wake each morning to the sound of birds,
And the smell of coffee brewing in the air.
On my porch, I witness the sun's rise,
Feeling peace and joy, as the world comes alive.

I go for a walk in the woods,
And I feel the sun on my face and the wind in my hair.
I see the beauty of nature,
And I am filled with gratitude.

I come home and make a simple meal,
And I enjoy it with my loved ones.
We laugh and talk,
And I feel connected to them.

Night falls, I gaze at the stars above,
I am filled with awe and wonder,
Grateful for life's gifts, big and small,
Simple things, blessings for us all.

The simple things in life are often the
most joyful.
They are the things that bring us peace,
Gratitude, and connection.

CHAPTER I: DAILY LIFE

So let us not take them for granted.
Let us cherish them,
And let them fill our lives with joy.

Taking on the Day

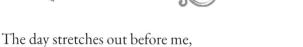

The day stretches out before me,
A blank canvas, a clean page.
I can paint it with anything,
With joy or with regrets.

I can choose to be idle,
To let the day pass me by.
Or I can choose to be productive,
To make the most of every minute.

The choice is mine,
And it is up to me
To decide how I will fill
This precious gift of time.

So I will choose to be brave,
To take on the day with courage.
I will not let fear or doubt
Hold me back from achieving my goals.

I will embrace the unknown,
And I will face each challenge head-on.
I will not give up,
No matter how difficult things may seem.

CHAPTER I: DAILY LIFE

I will keep going,
Until I reach my goal.
And when I do,
I will know that I have lived this day to the fullest.

The Work-Life Balance

Balancing work and life, a delicate line,
A dance we all strive to intertwine.
Excessive work leads to fast burnout,
Too much play, stability in doubt.

The key lies in finding a harmonious space,
Where productivity meets inner grace.
It's challenging, yet worth the quest,
To say, "I've truly lived," when we reflect.

Take time for yourself, don't hesitate,
Recharge, unwind, embrace the tranquil state.
But remember to work hard, dedicated and true,
For without effort, our dreams won't come into view.

Monday Motivation

Monday, oh Monday, here I come!
With coffee in hand and spirits high,
Ready to conquer, ready to thrive.

I know challenges await, but I won't back down,
Work hard, have fun, wear success like a crown.

Bring it on, Monday, I'm ready, it's true,
This week will be my best, goals I'll pursue.

Making a difference, my aim each day,
No obstacle can hinder, success is my name.

No barriers can block my way,
I'll embrace the journey, come what may.

Monday, be ready, I'm charging ahead,
With determination and passion, I'll forge ahead.

So watch out, Monday!
Here I come!

Chapter 2:

The Journey of Life

CHAPTER 2: THE JOURNEY OF LIFE

Birth and Childhood

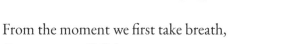

From the moment we first take breath,
Our journey of life begins.
With tiny fingers, and little feet,
And wonder in our eyes, so wide and deep.

We journey through our childhood years,
With innocence and joy, and childish fears.
We run and play, with laughter and song,
Our spirits free, and our hearts full and strong.

The world is a playground, and life is a game,
Filled with adventures and discoveries, so new and so strange.
We chase the butterflies, and catch fireflies in a jar,
And the sun sets slowly, as our childhood fades to a star.

We learn to love, and we learn to lose,
We make friends, and we pick our shoes.
We grow taller, and stronger, and more wise,
And our journey of life, before our very eyes.

So hold tight to your memories, of your childhood days,
And cherish the moments, in your heart and in your ways.
For they will always be with you, through the highs and through the lows,
And they will guide you, through your journey of life, wherever it goes.

Coming of Age

Life's journey is a winding road,
With twists and turns we must go.
From innocence and childhood dreams,
To facing reality's harsh beams.

We set out with youthful fire,
Our hearts aflame with pure desire,
To conquer all, to reach the sky,
With courage, hope, and bravery high.

But as we travel through life's stage,
We encounter obstacles and rage,
That threaten to break our spirit,
And leave us lost and in a slits.

Yet we rise again, stronger, bolder,
With scars that make us all the colder,
For they are the tales we must share,
The stories of how we came to care.

And so, the journey goes on,
Through valleys low and peaks so long,
With each step we find our way,
To wisdom, peace, and come of age.

CHAPTER 2: THE JOURNEY OF LIFE

For life is not a destination,
But a journey of transformation,
From ignorance to understanding,
From youth to maturity, expanding.

So embrace the road ahead,
With open arms and heart full of red,
For it is the journey of a lifetime,
The story of our becoming, sublime.

Falling in Love

Life is a journey, a path that we tread,
With ups and downs, and hills to be climbed,
But it is not the destination we're led,
It's the memories we make, the love we find.

As we walk this road, we search for our truth,
We look for the light that will guide us along,
And in the darkness, a star shines anew,
A love that is pure, a love that is strong.

It's like the first rain after a long drought,
A thirst quenching shower that revives the earth,
It's like the sun breaking through a heavy cloud,
A warm embrace after a long winter's dearth.

It's like a butterfly emerging from its cocoon,
A metamorphosis, a transformation complete,
It's like the moon reflecting on a calm lagoon,
A serene beauty that steals away our breath.

So let us hold on to this love, dear friends,
For it is a treasure, a gift from the universe,
And in this journey of life, until its end,
It will be our beacon, our guiding dove.

CHAPTER 2: THE JOURNEY OF LIFE

For love is the thread that binds us all,
A bond that transcends time and space,
And as we journey on, through life's falls,
It will be our anchor, our saving grace.

Getting Married

In the fields of love, where the daisies sway,
With the sun shining bright, and the birds at play,
Two hearts beat as one, in the sweetest way.
As they take the vows, that will change their day.

With the ring of gold, shining like the sun,
And the kiss of love, that has just begun,
Their souls entwine, in a bond so true,
And the world around them, just fades from view.

The fragrance of love, fills the summer air,
With the rustling leaves, and the laughter so fair,
And the twirling dance, of two hearts in glee,
Under the stars, in a sky so free.

The vows they took, in that sacred hour,
With the love they share, like a sweet summer shower,
And the life they lead, from that day on,
Will be filled with love, till the break of dawn.

So let us celebrate, this love so pure,
With the laughter and joy, that will ever endure,
For the two hearts beating, as one, today,
Are the symbols of love, that will never fade away.

Blessings Unfold

Tiny hands that fit so snug in ours,
Eyes that sparkle like celestial stars,
Innocence written in every curve,
A love that forever will serve.

Their laughter like music to our ears,
A symphony wiping away our tears,
With each giggle, our hearts take flight,
And we're grateful for this joyous sight.

Watching them grow, a wondrous thing,
Their personalities, a gift they bring,
From crawling to walking, learning to play,
Our love for them blossoms each day.

Like a garden, they bloom with grace,
Their beauty a smile on our face,
And though they may wander, they'll always return,
To the home where their roots forever burn.

So hold tight to these blessings untold,
For soon they'll grow wings and soar so bold,
But in our hearts, they'll always remain,
The children who brought us endless joy and gain.

Chapter 3:

The Power of Love

The First Meeting

Two souls, once unknown,
In a crowded room, alone.
Eyes met, hearts skipped a beat,
A spark, so rare and sweet.

The air grew thick with mystery,
Electricity, pure alchemy.
A smile, a nod, a gentle touch,
And love, it flowed, like a rushing stream.

The sun, it set, in a sky of gold,
As they walked, hand in hand, so bold.
Their laughter, like chimes, filled the air,
As they whispered secrets, without a care.

The stars, they twinkled, like diamonds bright,
As they made their way, into the night.
And the moon, it shone, like a beacon of love,
Guiding them, to their destiny above.

From that moment on, they knew,
That their hearts, forever, would be true.
For in that first meeting, they found,
A love, so pure, so rare, so profound.

So, when you find that special one,
In a crowded room, or in the sun,
Hold on tight, and never let go,
For love, it's a journey, that's meant to grow.

The Promise of a Lifetime

Underneath the starry skies,
Where the moonlight dances and sighs,
We made a promise, you and I,
To love each other until we die.

Our hearts beat as one, like the waves,
Crashing against the shore, in perfect rhythm and waves,
Our love, a fire, burning bright,
Illuminating the darkness of the night.

Like the petals of a rose,
Soft and delicate, yet strong and bold,
Our love blossoms, forever growing,
Nourished by the words we keep sharing and knowing.

Like the branches of an ancient tree,
Our love roots deep, for all eternity,
Providing shelter, in life's stormy weather,
Together, we face it, now and forever.

In the stillness of the night,
We hold each other, oh so tight,
Whispering sweet nothings, in each other's ear,
The promise of a lifetime, my dear.

So let us dance, under the moonlight,
Holding hands, until the morning light,
For our love, a beautiful sight,
Is the promise of a lifetime, shining bright.

The Gift of Partnership

Love is a rose, delicate and fair,
Its petals soft, its fragrance rare.
A beauty to behold, a joy to possess,
A treasure to nurture, a promise to confess.

And when two hearts are joined as one,
The rose blooms brighter, its beauty shines on.
For love is not just a single stem,
But a garden of joy, where two hearts blend.

Together they tend the soil and the rain,
Nourishing the love, banishing the pain.
And as the seasons come and go,
Their love grows stronger, its roots aglow.

For love is not just a moment in time,
But a journey to cherish, a climb to the sublime.
And in each other's arms, they find
The strength to face life, to be loving and kind.

The sun and the moon, day and night,
Two hearts beating as one, shining bright.
A symphony of love, a dance so divine,
The gift of partnership, a love so fine.

So hold on tight, to the one you adore,
For love is a rose, that will bloom forevermore.
A treasure to cherish, a bond to keep,
The gift of partnership, a love so deep.

CHAPTER 3: THE POWER OF LOVE

The Beauty of Relationships

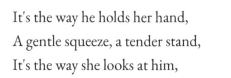

It's the way he holds her hand,
A gentle squeeze, a tender stand,
It's the way she looks at him,
With eyes that shine and never dim.

It's the laughter that fills the room,
A sound so sweet, a blissful boom,
It's the silly jokes they share,
That only they can understand.

It's the way they dance in rain,
With joy and love, without restrain,
It's the way they chase the sun,
Together, forever as one.

It's the way they comfort each,
With love and care, beyond reach,
It's the way they stand the test,
Of life's rough winds, at their best.

It's the way they build their nest,
With dreams and hopes, at their best,
It's the way they grow as one,
In love that shines, like the sun.

It's the way they face the night,
With courage, strength, and all their might,
It's the way they chase the dawn,
Together, forever as one.

It's the beauty of relationships,
A bond so pure, beyond depths,
It's the magic of love's art,
That beats within, every heart.

So cherish it, hold it tight,
This love so bright, with all your might,
For it's the beauty of life's dance,
In the warmth of relationships, a chance.

The Power of Love

Love is a river, wild and free,
Flowing with grace and energy,
It winds its way through life's rough terrain,
Bringing joy and healing to the pain.

It's a rose that blooms in the harshest of climates,
A lighthouse that guides us through life's troubled tides,
It's a bond that ties two hearts as one,
A symphony that's forever begun.

It's a fire that burns with a passionate heat,
A treasure more valuable than any diamond or gold,
It's a balm that soothes the soul's deepest pain,
A journey that takes us home again.

Love is a wonder, a creation of our hearts,
A power that transforms and uplifts,
It's a bird that takes flight on wings of grace,
A miracle that brightens every place.

So hold tight to the power of love,
Let its light guide you on your way,
For it's the one thing that will never depart,
And will always be with you come what may.

Chapter 4:

The Aging Journey

CHAPTER 4: THE AGING JOURNEY

The Golden Years

The leaves on the trees, once green and bright,
Now turn to a golden hue, a sight to behold.
A symphony of colours, a reminder bold,
Of the stories yet to be told.

The winds of time, a gentle breeze,
Carry with them memories and keys.
To a world of laughter, of love and of pain,
Of sunsets and dawns, of rain and of gain.

The wrinkles on our skin, a road map of our lives,
A story of joy, of laughter, of tears and strife.
Each line a chapter, each chapter a tale,
Of the journey we've taken, the bridges we've sailed.

The silver in our hair, a crown of the wise,
A symbol of the battles we've won and the skies.
We've gazed upon, of the dreams we've let go,
Of the laughter and love, that continue to flow.

So let us embrace these golden years,
With grace and with joy, with laughter and tears.
For each day is a blessing, a gift from the universe,
A journey to cherish, a tale of love.

And when our time comes, to leave this earth,
We'll leave behind a legacy, of immeasurable worth.
A story of love, of laughter, of life well lived,
A story to be told, of the golden years we give.

CHAPTER 4: THE AGING JOURNEY

The Art of Growing Older

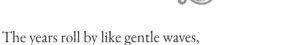

The years roll by like gentle waves,
Crashing softly on the shore,
A tapestry of memories,
Woven with love evermore.

The wrinkles on our face,
A roadmap of our lives,
Each line a story told,
Of joy and pain and strife.

Our hair turns silver, like the moon,
Reflecting all we've known,
Our eyes hold the wisdom,
Of seasons come and gone.

Our bodies may slow down,
But our spirit soars on high,
The art of growing older,
Is learning how to fly.

We plant our roots deep,
In the soil of our past,
Nourishing our soul,
For the journey that will last.

We are like the oak tree,
Strong and steadfast we stand,
Our branches reaching skyward,
Embracing life's demands.

So let us dance in the sun,
And sing in the rain,
For the art of growing older,
Is to cherish life again.

So hold on to your dreams,
And never let them die,
For the art of growing older,
Is the beauty of the sky.

CHAPTER 4: THE AGING JOURNEY

Reflections on Time

Time, the thief of youth, creeps in unannounced,
Stealing moments, memories, and years.
It leaves behind wrinkles, greying hair, and pain,
And a heart that beats with a slower pace.

But with each passing day, I see more clearly,
The beauty in the journey, the wisdom in the scars.
The laughter and tears, the love and the loss,
All woven together in a tapestry of life.

The sun rises and sets, marking the hours,
And the moon waxes and wanes, reflecting my soul.
I am but a traveller, on a path ever winding,
With each step, I leave behind a footprint in the sand.

I see the world through different eyes,
With a deeper appreciation for the simple things,
The rustle of leaves, the chirp of birds,
And the warm embrace of the morning sun.

I've learned to cherish the now, to live in the moment,
To laugh often, love deeply, and never look back.
For time is a river, that flows ever onward,
And I am but a leaf, carried along by its current.

So I embrace each day, with open arms and an open heart,
And hold tight to the memories, that make me who I am.
For time may be the thief of youth, but it is also the giver of grace,
And I am grateful for the journey, and the reflections on time.

CHAPTER 4: THE AGING JOURNEY

The Wisdom of Age

As the years pass by,
Our lives unfold,
A tapestry of joy,
Love and strife.

Wrinkles and silver hair
Are symbols of our wisdom,
Worn like a badge of honour
For all the years we've lived.

Like the bark on a tree,
We've weathered life's storms,
And our roots have grown strong
Through the tests we've faced.

We've learned to bend, not break,
In the face of adversity,
And our scars are a testament
To our strength and resilience.

The setting sun casts a golden glow
On our faces,
A reminder of the beauty
That time can bring.

We've seen the changing seasons,
The ebb and flow of life,
And we've learned to cherish each moment,
For it may be the last.

Like the stars in the sky,
Our memories shine bright,
Guiding us through life's journey,
Both day and night.

We've learned to love deeply,
To forgive, and to be kind,
And these are the gifts
That the wisdom of age brings.

So let us embrace the wisdom of age,
And the rich tapestry of life that it brings.
For with each passing year,
We become more wise,
And our life's story continues to unfold before our eyes.

Embracing the Journey

As the years pass by, and the wrinkles deepen,
And the hair turns silver, like the moonlight gleaming,
We are reminded that life is a fleeting dream,
And we must cherish every moment, every beam.

The journey of age, though sometimes slow and weary,
Is a path that we must all one day embrace,
With grace and dignity, and a heart full of cheer,
As we navigate the ups and downs of life's race.

Like the leaves that fall from the branches of trees,
And the petals that wilt from the flowers of the field,
We too must one day let go of our youth,
And surrender to the beauty of age revealed.

But though our bodies may grow old and tired,
Our spirit remains young, wild and free,
With memories of laughter, love and joy,
That light up the darkness and set our hearts aglow.

So let us embrace the journey, with open arms,
And dance to the rhythm of life's symphony,
For each step we take, and each breath we take,
Is a precious gift, a blessing from the universe.

And as we journey on, through the twists and turns,
And the highs and lows, of life's endless road,
Let us hold on to hope, and to love,
For these are the gifts, that light our way home.

Chapter 5:

Breaking Free from Stereotypes

Unique Reflections

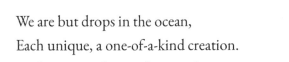

We are but drops in the ocean,
Each unique, a one-of-a-kind creation.
With our own hopes, fears, and passions,
Our individuality a powerful manifestation.

Like the colours in a kaleidoscope,
We reflect light in our own ways.
Some may shine brighter, some may fade,
But each one holds its own brilliance and grace.

We are like the leaves on a tree,
Each with its own shape and hue.
Some are bold and bright, some are meek,
But all are necessary for the tree to grow true.

And like the stars in the night sky,
We each have our own story to tell.
Some may twinkle brighter, some may lie,
But each one contributes to the celestial spell.

So embrace your individuality,
Embrace the person you were meant to be.
For like a butterfly emerging from its cocoon,
You'll find strength in the person you'll soon become.

So spread your wings and fly high,
And never be afraid to let your light shine.
For in this world of sameness and conformity,
Your individuality is a rare gem of true beauty.

Unchained Beauty

In a world that tells us to conform,
To fit into boxes, to be like the norm,
We often forget the beauty within,
The unique qualities that make us grin.

Like a wildflower, unapologetically bold,
Rising tall, breaking through the mould,
Its petals soft, its colours bright,
Its fragrance a symbol of its might.

So too, we must embrace our own,
The quirks, the imperfections, the unknown,
For it is in these traits that we find,
The strength of individuality, one of a kind.

Like a river carving its path through the earth,
Defying the boundaries, giving birth,
To new perspectives, new ways of life,
Its journey a testament to inner strife.

So let us not be afraid to be ourselves,
To let our light shine, to break from the shelves,
For in doing so, we will find what's true,
The power of individuality, shining through.

So embrace the wildflower, the river's might,
And remember, it's okay to shine bright,
For the strength of individuality, cannot be tamed,
It is the source of inspiration, the driving flame.

Individuality

I am a river, wild and free,
Flowing through life with mystery,
My currents strong, my spirit bold,
The journey of self, a story untold.

I am a tree, tall and proud,
Reaching for the sky, unbound,
My roots deep, my branches high,
A symbol of strength against the sky.

I am the wind, blowing with might,
Carving my path, shining so bright,
With every gust, I spread my wings,
Embracing life, with all its things.

I am the sun, shining so warm,
Guiding the way, through night and storm,
My rays of light, a beacon bright,
Illuminating the path to what's right.

For I am unique, and so are you,
With gifts and talents, that only few,
Can boast of having, and so we must,
Embrace our individuality, and trust.

In the journey of self-discovery,
We must have faith, and be bold and merry,
For the strength of individuality,
Lies in embracing who we are truly.

So let us be proud, of who we are,
And let our light, shine like a star,
For in this world, so full of grace,
The strength of individuality, shines in every face.

CHAPTER 5: BREAKING FREE FROM STEREOTYPES

The Power of Social Influence

We're but mere leaves, on a windswept tree,
Tossed and turned, by society's sea.
Our thoughts and actions, shaped by its might,
The power of influence, a guiding light.

We dance to the beat, of what others say,
Our identity, lost in the fray.
Conformity reigns, in this endless throng,
Our true selves, forgotten and gone.

But what if we dared, to break free from the mould,
To shed our disguise, and let our souls unfold?
What if we found, the courage within,
To forge our own path, and let our hearts sing?

The journey is hard, and the road is unclear,
But the prize is great, and the reward is dear.
For in discovering, our authentic selves,
We unleash the power, of true wealth.

The power to love, and to be loved in return,
The power to live, and to truly yearn.
The power to soar, above society's fray,
The power to be, who we were meant to be each day.

So take a deep breath, and close your eyes,
And listen to the whispers, of your soul's cries.
For within you lies, a world yet untold,
The power to be, more than just a leaf on the windswept fold.

Breaking Free

In the depths of our mind, we search for our light
To guide us on our journey through the night
But oftentimes, we're swayed by those around us
By the opinions and beliefs, they make a fuss

We look to the right, we look to the left
And wonder if we're living our life correct
But the truth is, our path is our own to take
And the power to choose, we have to make

We're like delicate flowers, swaying in the breeze
Bending to the will of the winds, as they tease
But the beauty of a flower, lies in its own bloom
And not in the shadows, it casts in its room

So why do we let the world, shape who we are
When the only voice that matters, is the one from our heart
Why do we follow, when we should lead the way
Why do we let others, dictate what we say

It's time to shed the chains, that hold us back
And let the power of self, be the guiding track
To discover the beauty, that lies within
And let the world see, the true person we've been

So take a deep breath, and take a step forward
Embrace the journey, and let your spirit soar
For the power of social influence, is just a myth
And the only true power, lies within your own self.

Discovering Self

Like a seed planted deep in the earth,
A soul takes root, with endless worth.
A journey starts, to find its own,
A path to follow, a heart to hone.

Through sun and rain, wind and snow,
It grows and blossoms, with strength aglow.
A sapling becomes a towering tree,
Its branches reaching, so wild and free.

The trunk is sturdy, the roots entwine,
A foundation strong, of self and time.
A beacon shining, in the night,
A symbol of hope, with all its might.

The leaves rustle, with every breeze,
Whispers of memories, and moments to seize.
The fruit it bears, so sweet and bright,
A reflection of all that is right.

So look within, and find the seed,
The spark of life, that you truly need.
Nurture it well, and let it grow,
To a beautiful tree, with its own unique glow.

For the strength of personal identity,
Is found in the journey, of self-discovery.
Embrace the journey, and find your way,
To the person you were meant to be, every day.

Chapter 6:

Discovering Your True Self

CHAPTER 6: DISCOVERING YOUR TRUE SELF

The Path to Self-Discovery

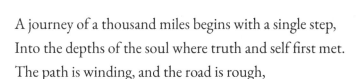

A journey of a thousand miles begins with a single step,
Into the depths of the soul where truth and self first met.
The path is winding, and the road is rough,
But the destination is worth all the pain and the struggle.

Like the sun breaking through the clouds after a stormy night,
Discovering oneself brings a new and brilliant light.
It illuminates the shadows of the heart and the mind,
And sets the spirit free, of all doubts and fears left behind.

It's a quest that takes us to the mountains and the sea,
To the valleys and the rivers, where the answers wait for thee.
It's a pilgrimage that leads us to the gardens of the soul,
Where the flowers of our true selves, forever more unfold.

It's a dance with the winds that blows away the veil,
Revealing the beauty and the power that always will prevail.
It's a symphony that echoes through the halls of time,
As we discover the melodies of our own divine rhyme.

The power of self-discovery lies within us all,
A treasure trove of knowledge, waiting to be uncovered and shown.
So, heed the call of the heart, and embark on the quest,

THE JOURNEY TO SELF-LOVE

For the greatest adventure of all, is the journey of self-test.

And as you walk the path, and as you reach the end,
You'll find that you are not lost, but exactly where you've been.
For the answers were within you, all along the way,
And the power of self-discovery, is yours to keep and to play.

Self-Expression

Amidst the roar of societal norms,
Where conformity takes its form,
I wander through the maze of life,
In search of my true self, devoid of strife.

A journey through a world so vast,
Where masks are worn, not meant to last,
And in the depths of my soul I delve,
To find my voice, my truth to tell.

Like a butterfly emerging from its chrysalis,
I shed my skin and embrace my prowess,
I spread my wings and take to flight,
With a newfound strength, a new sight.

For I am the canvas on which I paint,
A masterpiece of my own design,
With each brush stroke, I come alive,
And my spirit soars, unbridled and bright.

The colours of my soul, I lay bare,
For all to see, without a care,
For in self-expression, I find my might,
And the courage to face each coming night.

So let my voice ring out, clear and bold,
A symphony of my being untold,
For in the strength of self-expression,
Lies the power of true self-possession.

CHAPTER 6: DISCOVERING YOUR TRUE SELF

The Freedom to Be Yourself

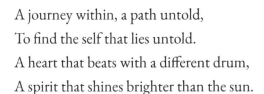

A journey within, a path untold,
To find the self that lies untold.
A heart that beats with a different drum,
A spirit that shines brighter than the sun.

In search of answers, in search of truth,
We wander aimlessly in our youth.
But as we grow and as we learn,
We start to see what we yearn.

It's not the praise of others we seek,
But the peace that lies within, so unique.
A journey to love the self we are,
To cast aside the false shining star.

It's not the mask we wear with pride,
But the raw and vulnerable soul inside.
The freedom to be who we truly are,
To let our true colours shine like a shooting star.

And as we embrace the imperfection,
We find the beauty in our reflection.
A light that shines, a strength that's real,
A love for self that we can truly feel.

So take a step, take a breath,

And trust the journey to self-acceptance.

For in this freedom, we truly soar,

And find the peace that we've been searching for.

Self-Realization

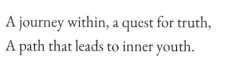

A journey within, a quest for truth,
A path that leads to inner youth.
A quest for answers, a search for light,
A journey that helps us see what's right.

It starts with a whisper, a gentle call,
A voice that beckons, and gives us all,
The courage to leave behind our fears,
And face the unknown, with hopes and tears.

We walk a path, that's rough and steep,
And every step, we learn to leap,
Over boulders of doubt and streams of pain,
Towards a brighter future, that's not in vain.

We reach a summit, and there we stand,
Gazing at the view, of our own land,
And there we see, what we couldn't see,
The beauty of life, and the mystery.

We see our past, and all its scars,
And learn to forgive, and let go of bars,
We see our present, and all its gifts,
And learn to cherish, and embrace its thrifts.

And finally, we see our future bright,
And all its possibilities, in its sight,
And learn to trust, and take the leap,
Towards a life, of endless bliss and peace.

So take a step forward, with courage and grace,
And let the journey of self-discovery take place,
For when we find ourselves, we'll find the world,
And a life filled with meaning, purpose, and joy unfurled.

The Promise of Personal Growth

It starts with a seed, small and shy,
Beneath the soil, where light cannot reach the sky.
Yet it dreams and stretches, reaching for the sun,
With the promise of growth, and all that it can become.

Like the seed, we too begin small,
With aspirations, doubts, and fears that enthral.
But as we grow, our eyes come to see,
The beauty in the journey, and the mystery.

We wander through valleys, deep and still,
Where shadows linger, and doubts linger still.
But with each step, we find the might,
To rise above it all, and take flight.

We dance in fields, where flowers bloom,
With joy and laughter, and a heart full of room.
We bask in sunbeams, warm and bright,
And bask in the knowledge, that everything will be alright.

We climb the mountains, tall and grand,
With the wind at our backs, and a soul that's unbranded
We stand at the top, and look down below,
And realize the beauty, of the places we've come to know.

So let us embrace the journey of self-discovery,
With open hearts and minds, and a sense of bravery.
For within us all, lies the promise of growth,
And the chance to soar, and reach for what's both.

So let us be like the seed, small yet bold,
And follow the path, that leads to the gold.
For the journey of self-discovery, is a wondrous thing,
And the promise of personal growth, is the gift that it brings.

CHAPTER 7:

LOVING YOURSELF

The Beauty of Self-Love

In the mirror, I see a reflection,
Of a face that's etched with imperfections.
Lines that tell the story of my life,
Of laughter and tears, and joy and strife.

I see eyes that sparkle like the stars,
And a smile that brightens up my scars.
I see hair that dances in the wind,
And a spirit that's free, and unconfined.

And I know, in this moment of truth,
That the beauty I see, is not just youth.
It's the grace that comes with self-acceptance,
And the peace that comes with self-love's presence.

For when I look beyond the surface,
I see the soul that shines with purpose.
I see the heart that beats with passion,
And the courage that fuels my action.

And I realize, with a sudden blaze,
That the beauty I seek, I already possess.
It's within me, it's always been there,
A light that shines bright, beyond compare.

So I embrace the person I see,
With all their flaws and imperfections, wild and free.
And I celebrate the journey of self-discovery,
And the path that leads to self-love's recovery.

For in this journey, I've come to know,
That the beauty of self-love, begins with letting go.
Letting go of the fears, and the doubts, and the pain,
And embracing the truth, that we're all beautiful, just the same.

So I raise my head, and I stand tall,
And I bask in the light, of self-love's glow.
For I am worthy, and I am enough,
And the beauty of self-love, is simply beautiful.

CHAPTER 7: LOVING YOURSELF

The Power of Self-Worth

We are but a reflection
Of our thoughts and beliefs,
And the beauty we possess
Is not found in skin or shape.

It's the voice that speaks with kindness
And the courage to be true,
It's the love that we embrace
And the light that shines through.

The mountains we climb within
Are greater than any peak,
And the battles we win
Are the ones that make us strong.

So let the waves crash around
And the winds howl in the night,
For our self-worth knows no bounds
And our spirit takes flight.

Like the sun that rises high
And shines upon the earth,
Our self-worth touches the sky
And gives us a new birth.

THE JOURNEY TO SELF-LOVE

So hold your head up high
And let your spirit soar,
For the power of self-worth
Is something to adore.

Embrace the beauty within
And let your light shine bright,
For the power of self-worth
Is the greatest gift in sight.

CHAPTER 7: LOVING YOURSELF

The Strength of Self-Confidence

In the mirror, I once saw a stranger,
A soul burdened with self-doubt and anger.
But then I learned to look beyond,
And found the strength I needed to grow.

Like a blooming flower in a field of thorns,
I stood tall and proud, defying norms.
I let my true colours shine through,
And basked in the warmth of my newfound self-love.

For the scars that once brought me to my knees,
Are now the symbols of my victories.
And the voice that whispered I was not enough,
Is silenced by the roar of my self-acceptance.

I am the ocean, vast and unchanging,
With depths that hold my secrets and treasures.
I am the sky, a canvas of freedom,
With hues that paint my dreams and my pleasures.

I am enough, exactly as I am,
With flaws and imperfections and all.
For the strength of self-confidence comes from within,
And it gives me the courage to be myself.

So let us all learn to love ourselves,
And celebrate the beauty of our own skin.
For when we embrace who we truly are,
We unlock the power of self-confidence, a shining star.

CHAPTER 7: LOVING YOURSELF

The Freedom of Self-Forgiveness

I stood before the mirror,
Staring at my reflection.
A stranger's face I saw,
Filled with self-dissection.

Each flaw, each scar,
A cruel reminder of my past.
A heavy burden that held me captive,
Unable to move or breathe.

But then I closed my eyes,
And took a deep, calming breath.
I felt the weight of my doubts and fears begin to lessen,
And in that quiet moment,
I heard the voice of truth.

Whispering softly,
"You are enough."

I opened my eyes,
And saw a different image in the glass.
A person strong and resilient,
With scars that tell a story.

A tale of survival and perseverance,
Of battles fought and won.
A life of purpose,
With light shining bright,
Like a rising sun.

And in that moment,
I forgave myself for all my wrongs.
I let go of the past,
And embraced the present moment.

I accepted all my flaws,
And celebrated my unique qualities.
For I am more than just the sum of my mistakes.

I am a work of art,
With threads of gold and silver woven in.
A creation of beauty,
With endless potential within.

I am worthy of love,
And deserving of peace.
For I am enough,
Just as I am,
In all my complexities.

CHAPTER 7: LOVING YOURSELF

So I will stand before the mirror,
With my head held high.
And smile at the reflection,
With no need to disguise.

For I have found the freedom,
Of self-forgiveness and grace.
And in that acceptance,
I have found my rightful place.

The Miracle of Self-Acceptance

In a world that tells us we're not enough,
We hide behind a mask, so tough.
We strive for perfection, we chase a dream,
But forget that beauty lies within the seams.

We fixate on flaws and criticize our hue,
But the miracle of self-acceptance shines through.
It's the realization that we are unique,
That our quirks and imperfections make us complete.

Like a garden full of flowers, each one unique,
Our individuality is what makes us chic.
And just like a butterfly breaking free,
We too can embrace our authenticity.

So let's stop hiding behind our masks,
And start celebrating who we are.
Let's let go of the need for perfection,
And embrace our own unique beauty.

With self-acceptance, comes a peaceful mind,
A heart that's full of love, and a soul that's kind.
It's the power to love ourselves, just as we are,
To bask in the beauty of who we are.

CHAPTER 7: LOVING YOURSELF

When we accept ourselves, we open the door to a life of joy,
A life of love, and a life of peace.
We are no longer bound by the expectations of others,
We are free to be ourselves.

So let us embrace our uniqueness,
Let us celebrate our imperfections,
And let us love ourselves, unconditionally.
For when we do, we will truly experience the miracle of self-acceptance.

CHAPTER 8:

FINDING PURPOSE AND MEANING

CHAPTER 8: FINDING PURPOSE AND MEANING

New Dawns and Fresh Starts

The morning sun rises, a new day begins,
A blank canvas waiting to be filled in.
A chance to leave the past behind,
To start anew, and be re-defined.

The dew on the grass glistens like diamonds,
A symbol of the purity of new beginnings.
The breeze blows softly, carrying hope,
Whispering to us, it's time to cope.

The birds sing a melody so sweet,
Their joyous tunes cannot be beat.
They remind us that life is a song,
And it's never too late to right what's wrong.

The sky is ablaze with hues of pink and gold,
A breathtaking sight, worth more than gold.
It speaks of the beauty that lies ahead,
And the promise of happiness, that can't be misled.

So let us embrace this brand new day,
With open arms, and hearts that sway.
Let us leave behind all our fears,
And chase our dreams, through the coming years.

For every sunrise brings a fresh start,
An opportunity to heal a broken heart.
To find new purpose, and soar like a dove,
And discover the wonders of life, that we're yet to love.

The Journey Through Life

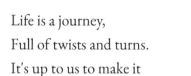

Life is a journey,
Full of twists and turns.
It's up to us to make it
A journey worth the burns.

We'll face challenges,
But we'll also find joy.
We'll make mistakes,
But we'll learn from them, too.

We'll meet new people,
And we'll say goodbye to old.
We'll experience the best
And the worst that life has to hold.

But through it all,
We'll grow and change.
We'll become the people
We were meant to be.

So let's embrace this journey,
With all its ups and downs.
Let's make the most of it,
And live our lives to the fullest.

The Meaning of Life

Where is the meaning of life to be found?
In the beating of a drum,
The rhythm of the rain,
The rolling of the thunder?

Or is it hidden in the petals of a rose,
The beauty of a sunset hue,
The smile of a newborn child,
That shines a light so true?

Perhaps it is woven in the fabric of the stars,
The mystery of the Milky Way,
The wonder of a universe,
That stretches far away.

Or is it simply in the moments,
That we share with those we hold dear,
In the laughter and the tears,
The push and pull of life so clear?

The meaning of life is not something that can be found,
It is something that must be made.
It is a journey that we all must take,
A quest that is ours alone.

So let us not search for the meaning of life,
But rather let us create it.
Let us fill our lives with moments of joy,
And let us cherish the ones we love.

For the meaning of life is not something that can be found,
It is something that we make.
And it is up to us to make it beautiful.

The Journey to Fulfilment

We wander through life like leaves in the breeze,
Adrift, searching for peace.
Our souls yearn for purpose, a reason to be,
A direction to follow, a path to see.

In the ocean of life, we are but drops,
Lost in the currents, searching for our thoughts.
But we must remember, we are not alone,
For every drop is a part of a greater whole.

The road ahead is long and unclear,
But we must forge ahead, never fearing.
For it is in the journey that we find,
The meaning of life, a peace of mind.

Like a bird soaring high in the sky,
We must spread our wings and learn to fly.
Embrace the unknown, take the leap of faith,
For it is only then that our purpose we'll trace.

The sun rises each day, a new chance to begin,
To chase our dreams and let our spirits spin.
The stars light our way, a guiding light,
Showing us the path to the mountains so bright.

And as we climb, each step we take,
Brings us closer to the fulfilment we make.
For it is not the destination that brings us joy,
But the journey that we take, our hearts to employ.

So let us dance in the rain, sing in the sun,
For it is in living that our purpose is won.
Embrace each day, each moment, each hour,
For it is in the journey that we find our power.

So take my hand, let us walk this road together,
Finding purpose and fulfilment, now and forever.
For it is in this journey that we will see,
The beauty of life, and what it means to be free.

The Gifts of Life Unseen

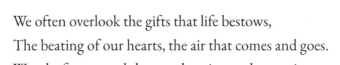

We often overlook the gifts that life bestows,
The beating of our hearts, the air that comes and goes.
We take for granted the sun that rises each morning,
And the rain that falls, to wash away life's burdens.

We fail to see the beauty in the laughter of a child,
Or the song of a bird in flight.
We forget the power of the colours of the earth,
And the love that binds us together.

We long for peace, but we fail to find it in the night,
Or in the memories we hold dear.
We miss the blessings in disguise,
That are all around us, if we would only look.

So let us open our eyes to the gifts of life,
No matter how small or seemingly insignificant.
Let us be grateful for the simple things,
And for the lessons we learn along the way.

For in these gifts, we find our true selves,
And our purpose in life.
They are the keys to our happiness,
And the foundation of our dreams.

CHAPTER 8: FINDING PURPOSE AND MEANING

So let us cherish the gifts of life,
And never take them for granted.
For they are the most precious things we have,
And they are the only things that truly matter.

CHAPTER 9:

OVERCOMING ADVERSITY

CHAPTER 9: OVERCOMING ADVERSITY

Rise Again

When life knocks you down, don't you dare stay there,
Stand tall, like a mighty oak tree with care.
Embrace the storm, let the winds blow,
For you are a warrior, with a heart aglow.

Like a phoenix from the ashes, rise and soar,
With wings of fire, reach for something more.
The road ahead may be long and steep,
But you have the strength to take that leap.

Like the sun that breaks through the clouds,
Shine bright, let your spirit be loud.
For every setback, every fall,
You'll rise again, stronger than all.

Like a river that never stops its flow,
Keep moving forward, don't let the current slow.
For in the journey of life, there will be twists and turns,
But with resilience, you'll conquer and learn.

So when life knocks you down, don't you ever give in,
Rise again, with a fire within.
For you are a champion, a warrior at heart,
With the strength and courage to play your part.

Embracing Change

Like leaves on a tree, we sway in the wind,
Never still, always shifting, changing skin.
Embrace the winds of change, let them blow,
For they bring growth, and help us grow.

The river flows, it never stays the same,
It moves forward, in a never-ending game.
It adapts to the rocks, and bends with the curves,
Embrace change, like the river that never preserves.

The clouds roll in, they shape shift and shift,
A reminder that change is a constant gift.
Embrace the storm, dance in the rain,
For it cleanses and washes away the pain.

The butterfly spreads its wings, and takes flight,
Leaving behind the cocoon, entering the light.
Embrace change, like the butterfly's metamorphosis,
For it brings new beginnings, and endless possibilities.

Change can be scary, and filled with unknowns,
But it leads to growth, and new frontiers to be shown.
Embrace change, with open arms and an open heart,
For it leads to self-discovery, a brand new start.

So let the winds of change, blow you where they may,
And trust the journey, for a better tomorrow and a brighter day.
Embrace change, and watch your world transform,
For change is the only constant, and is necessary to be reborn.

Turning Setbacks into Comebacks

When life deals a harsh blow,
And your dreams seem to be laid low,
Remember that setbacks can lead to comebacks,
And you can rise from the ashes like a phoenix.

Just like a seed that lies dormant in the earth,
Waiting for the right conditions to bring forth new birth,
So too can setbacks be the fertile ground,
That nurtures the seeds of greatness within.

Think of a wave that crashes to the shore,
Only to gather strength and rise up once more,
It is in the ebb and flow of life's tide,
That we find the courage to push forward and thrive.

Picture a butterfly emerging from its cocoon,
Breaking free from its limitations and constraints,
So too can setbacks be the catalyst,
That frees us from the limitations of our own minds.

So let us embrace the setbacks that we face,
For they are the building blocks of our comebacks,
And let us soar like eagles above the fray,
For in the face of adversity, we find our way.

CHAPTER 9: OVERCOMING ADVERSITY

Learning from Mistakes

Mistakes are the ink stains on our pages,
A blot upon the pristine white,
A crack within the marble statue,
A flaw that stands out to the sight.

But should we fear these errors,
These stumbling steps we take?
Or should we greet them with a smile,
And learn from our mistakes?

For when we falter, we discover
A new path we had not seen,
A hidden door that opens wide
To realms we've never been.

And when we stumble and we fall,
We learn to stand up tall,
For every bruise and every scar
Is a lesson to us all.

The beauty of life lies in the journey,
Where we learn from mistakes, and we grow,
For every twist and every turn
We'll emerge wiser, and more strong.

So when you feel lost, when you feel alone,
Remember, you're not on your own,
For every mistake you make,
You'll learn, and you'll break through.

And when you reach the end of your path,
You'll see that every mistake was a stepping-stone,
For you to become who you are,
A masterpiece of your own.

So embrace the unknown, and embrace your mistakes,
For they are the keys to the life you create,
And with every lesson that you take,
You'll soar higher, and you'll never break.

CHAPTER 9: OVERCOMING ADVERSITY

The Journey of Life

We are not meant to arrive
But to travel with the joy
Of the glistening sea,
The wind in our hair,
The sun on our faces.

We are not meant to reach the end
But to savour each moment
As we climb the mountain,
Cross the river,
Explore the valley.

We are not meant to find the answer
But to ask the question,
To seek the truth,
To grow in wisdom.

We are not meant to be perfect
But to be human,
To make mistakes,
To learn from them.

We are not meant to live in fear
But to live in love,

To embrace the unknown,
To trust the universe.

We are not meant to be alone
But to be connected,
To one another,
To the earth,
To the universe.

So let us travel together,
On this journey called life,
With joy in our hearts,
And love in our souls.

For we are not meant to arrive,
But to travel,
And the journey is the destination.

CHAPTER 9: OVERCOMING ADVERSITY

Sculpting Success in the Sands of Struggle

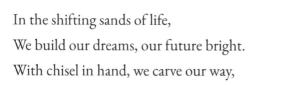

In the shifting sands of life,
We build our dreams, our future bright.
With chisel in hand, we carve our way,
Through mountains high and valleys low,
Through winds of change and storms of strife.

We are the artists of our own lives,
The sculptors of our own destiny.
We can create anything we set our minds to,
If we have the will and the determination.

The sands of struggle are our clay,
The canvas on which we create.
With every blow, we chip away,
The doubts and fears that hold us back.

With every step, we take a little closer,
To the masterpiece we are creating.
So let us not be afraid to struggle,
For it is through struggle that we grow.

Let us embrace the challenge,
And use it to make us stronger.
Let us not give up on our dreams,
No matter how hard things get.

For in the end, it is all worth it.
When we finally reach our goals,
We will look back and know that we have achieved something great.

We will have sculpted our own success,
From the sands of struggle.

Painting Futures on the Canvas of Time

With a brush dipped in dreams
And a palette of hues,
We paint our futures
On the canvas of time.

Each stroke a wish,
Each hue a desire,
We bring to life
The hopes we hold most dear.

The colours blend and swirl,
A symphony of light,
A masterpiece of what we yearn to see.

The future unfolds,
A tapestry of dreams,
A work of art
That's worth more than gold.

The canvas glows with the light of tomorrow,
A beacon of hope that shines bright,

A testament to all we dare to be,
A shining path for all to see.

So let us paint our futures,
With passion and with care,
And trust in the hand
That guides us there.

For each brush stroke is a step along the way,
And every colour holds the promise of a better day.

So let us paint our futures,
On the canvas of time,
And trust that our dreams will one day come true.
For each stroke of the brush is a step toward the light,
And each hue a symbol of the future's might.

CHAPTER 9: OVERCOMING ADVERSITY

The right time is now

The right time is now,
Not tomorrow, not next week,
Not when you have more money,
Not when you have more time.

The right time is now,
When you are feeling the fire,
When you are feeling the drive,
When you are feeling alive.

Don't wait for the perfect moment,
Because it will never come.
The perfect moment is now,
So seize it and make your dreams come true.

Don't be afraid to fail,
Because failure is a stepping stone to success.
Everyone fails,
But the most successful people
Are the ones who keep getting back up.

So don't wait for the right time,
The right time is now.
It's time to turn the dream into reality, it's your hour to shine.

Chapter 10:

Overcoming Fears and Anxieties

An Unwelcome Guest

I have a secret, a hidden struggle within me.
It resides in my mind, longing to break free.
Whispers in the night sow doubt and fear.
They say I'm not enough, that success is never near.

But I refuse to let them control my fate.
I reclaim my power, it's never too late.
I will conquer my inner shadows, step by step.
Taking back my life, no longer feeling inept.

I find strength within, nurturing my soul.
Embracing courage, making fear lose control.
Happiness becomes my guiding light.
With each passing day, I'll win the fight.

My inner battles may try, but I won't be confined.
I am the author of my life, leaving worries behind.
I grow stronger, braver every day.
Transcending my fears, finding my own way.

Facing Your Fears

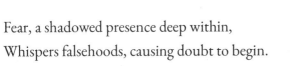

Fear, a shadowed presence deep within,
Whispers falsehoods, causing doubt to begin.
It tries to convince you that you're not strong,
That you're undeserving, that you don't belong.

But fear is a deceiver, a trickster in disguise,
It's time to confront it, to cut its ties.
Stand tall, show courage, let it know,
You're worthy of love, ready to grow.

You possess strength, you possess might,
You deserve happiness, to live in the light.
Don't let fear rule, don't let it control,
Take charge, be bold, and make fear's grip fold.

Fear is just an emotion, transient and fleeting,
It won't define you, its power depleting.
Step forward, face your fears with resolve,
Discover your potential, watch them dissolve.

Embrace life's journey, unburdened and free,
Fear won't hinder you, it's time to see.
You're capable, resilient, more than you know,
With each step forward, your confidence will grow.

So venture forth, seize life's grand call,
Fear won't hold you back, it'll be your downfall.
You're in command, the author of your fate,
Embrace your strength, for it's never too late.

The Courage to Be Yourself

To be yourself in a world
That wants to make you be someone else
Is the bravest thing that anyone can do.

It takes courage to stand up for what you believe in
Even when everyone else is telling you that you're wrong.
It takes courage to be different,
Even when it means being alone.

But it's worth it.
Because when you're true to yourself,
You're living your best life.

You're not wasting your time trying to be someone you're not.
You're not living in fear of what other people think.
You're not giving away your power.

You're owning your truth.
You're being your authentic self.
And that is the most beautiful thing in the world.

So don't be afraid to be yourself.
The world needs more of you.

The Fear of Rejection

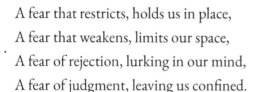

A fear that restricts, holds us in place,
A fear that weakens, limits our space,
A fear of rejection, lurking in our mind,
A fear of judgment, leaving us confined.

But we can rise above this fear,
We can confront it, make it disappear,
We can break free from its stifling hold,
And discover a life that's brave and bold.

For if we let fear dictate our way,
We'll never know what we could convey,
We'll miss out on joy, fulfilment, and bliss,
So let's release this fear, and seize our own bliss.

Let's face our doubts, let's make them small,
Embrace our worth, stand tall through it all,
Break the chains that keep us restrained,
Live fully, unburdened, no longer restrained.

So let's conquer our fear, let's set it free,
Embrace life's wonders, live authentically,
No longer held back, let's chase what's true,
With courage and love, our dreams we'll pursue.

CHAPTER 11:

THE IMPORTANCE OF FAMILY

The Love of a Parent

A parent's love is like a star,
Shining through the darkest of nights,
Guiding you through the storm and strife,
Bringing you to the dawn of light.

A parent's love is like a tree,
Rooted deep in the ground,
Providing shelter from the rain,
And protection from the cold.

A parent's love is like a river,
Flowing endlessly,
Never running dry,
Always there for you.

A parent's love is a gift,
One that is precious and rare,
A love that is unconditional,
A love that will never despair.

So cherish the love of your parents,
For it is a gift that is beyond compare,
A love that will last a lifetime,
A love that will never fade.

The Support of a Sibling

We are two trees, growing side by side,
Our roots intertwined, our branches high.
We share the sun, we share the rain,
We share the wind, we share the pain.

When one of us is weak, the other strong,
We lean upon each other for support.
We stand together, through the storm and night,
And face the future with a shared delight.

We are two trees, growing side by side,
Our roots intertwined, our branches high.
We are two siblings, bound by love,
Whose lives are intertwined above.

CHAPTER II: THE IMPORTANCE OF FAMILY

The Guidance of a Grandparent

A hand to hold and a heart to guide,
A smile to warm the darkest of times,
A love that knows no bounds or pride,
A wisdom beyond measure and rhyme.

A hand to help you up when you fall,
A heart to comfort you when you cry,
A smile to make you feel loved and cared for,
A love that will never deny.

A hand to hold you close and tight,
A heart to protect you from harm,
A smile to make you feel secure and safe,
A love that will never depart.

A hand to guide you through the years,
A heart to love you without fail,
A smile to make you feel cherished and special,
A love that will last until the end.

The Joy of a Child

A child's heart is a wondrous thing,
A wellspring of joy and delight,
A fountain of laughter and singing,
A rainbow of hope and delight.

It is a fragile thing,
A flower that needs careful tending,
A sapling that needs gentle supporting,
A firefly that needs sheltering.

But it is also a precious thing,
A gift from the universe,
A treasure to be cherished and loved,
A joy to behold and to love.

So let us nurture the hearts of children,
Let us protect them from harm,
Let us fill them with love and joy,
Let us give them the best possible start in life.

For in the hearts of children lies the future,
The hope of the world,
The promise of a better tomorrow.

CHAPTER 11: THE IMPORTANCE OF FAMILY

The Strength of a Family

A family is a circle of strength,
Where love and trust are the bonds of life;
And the children are the flowers of the wreath,
That binds the circle with beauty and strife.

The parents are the sun and the moon,
That shed their light on the path of the young;
And the home is the ark of safety,
Where the storms of life beat in vain on the strong.

The family is the foundation of the state,
And the strength of the nation is in the home;
And the future of the world is in the hands
Of the children who are growing up in the dome.

But a family is more than just a place,
It's a bond that can never be broken;
It's a love that can never be denied,
And a strength that can never be shaken.

So let us celebrate our families,
And cherish the bonds that we share;
For they are the foundation of our lives,
And the strength that will carry us through.

CHAPTER 12:

Healing

The Scar of Healing

The wound that bleeds is still the same,
No matter where it lies.
The pain is real, the hurt is same,
The tears will never dry.

The healing is a slow process,
With many ups and downs.
It takes time and patience,
And a lot of love around.

But when the healing is complete,
The scar will always remain.
A reminder of the pain,
But also of the gain.

The gain is strength and wisdom,
A new found appreciation
For life and all its beauty,
And the people in it.

Healing from Loss

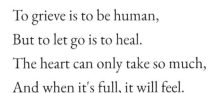

To grieve is to be human,
But to let go is to heal.
The heart can only take so much,
And when it's full, it will feel.

The pain is real, the loss is great,
But with time, it will fade.
The memories will stay with you,
But they will no longer make you afraid.

So grieve, but don't let it control your way,
Let tears flow, but don't let them stay.
And when ready, let go, find release,
Free yourself from anguish, find inner peace.

And heal.

CHAPTER 12: HEALING

Broken Heart

To heal the broken heart is not a task
So simple as to bind it up again.
For when the heart is broken, it doth ask
A deeper healing than the hands of men.

The heart that breaks is like a crystal vase
That falls and shatters on the marble floor.
The pieces cannot be put on again,
Nor can the vase be made as good as before.

But though the vase is broken, it may be
That from the fragments something new may spring.
A flower may grow, or a bird may build a nest,
And make the broken vase a thing of worth.

So when the heart is broken, it may be
That from the fragments something new may spring.
A new life may grow, or a new love may nestle,
And make the broken heart a thing of worth.

The Sun Has Left Me

The Sun has left me,
And the world is cold.
The days are dark,
And the nights are long.

I feel lost and alone,
Like a ship without a sail.
I don't know where to go,
Or how to find my way back home.

Yet, I'm not alone,
For the moon still shines,
And the stars still twinkle.
The rain still falls,
And the wind still blows.

And even though the sun is gone,
I know that it will return.
And when it does,
I will be ready.

I will be stronger,
And I will be wiser.

CHAPTER 12: HEALING

I will have learned from this experience,
And I will be a better person for it.

So even though the sun has left me,
I am not afraid.
I'll find my path, rediscover light,
Growing stronger, day by day.

The Loss of Love

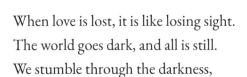

When love is lost, it is like losing sight.
The world goes dark, and all is still.
We stumble through the darkness,
Lost and alone.

But love is not dead.
It is only sleeping.
And like the sun after a winter storm,
It will rise again.

When love returns, it will be brighter than ever before.
It will fill our hearts with joy,
And light our way through the darkness.

So do not despair,
If love has left you.
It will come back to you,
When you least expect it.

And when it does,
You will be glad that you waited.

CHAPTER 13:

FINDING YOUR OWN PATH

CHAPTER 13: FINDING YOUR OWN PATH

The Search for Purpose

We seek our purpose,
A never-ending quest.
Always searching, never at rest.

Our minds wander,
Seeking meaning and worth,
A reason to thrive upon this Earth.

Yet, what if purpose is not a defined aim?
What if it's found in moments, not a claim?

Perhaps our purpose is to learn and grow,
To love and give, to let kindness show.

Maybe our purpose lies in making a change,
Leaving the world better in our own range.

Or perhaps our purpose is to find delight,
In the small moments, day and night.

Whatever our purpose may truly be,
Let's embrace the journey, live fully and free.

Fearlessly seek, strive, and explore,
For in living with purpose, we'll find more.

In the end, it's how we truly live,
That shapes our purpose and what we give.

The Quest for Happiness

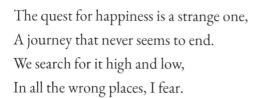

The quest for happiness is a strange one,
A journey that never seems to end.
We search for it high and low,
In all the wrong places, I fear.

We think that happiness is found
In wealth and fame and power.
But these things are fleeting,
And they can never bring true joy.

Happiness is found in the simple things,
In the love of family and friends.
It is found in the beauty of nature,
And in the peace of a quiet mind.

So if you are searching for happiness,
Look no further than your own heart.
It is there that you will find it,
Waiting for you to embrace it.

The Journey of Self-Discovery

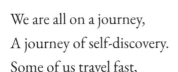

We are all on a journey,
A journey of self-discovery.
Some of us travel fast,
Some of us travel slow.

Some of us take the scenic route,
Some of us take the highway.
Some of us get lost,
Some of us find our way.

But no matter how we travel,
We all arrive at the same destination.
We all discover ourselves.

And when we do,
We are changed forever.
We are more whole,
We are more complete,
We are more ourselves.

So embrace your journey,
And enjoy the ride.
Self-discovery, a profound ride,
The most vital journey of your life.

The Gift of Hope

Hope is a gift that's hard to find,
For many do not know its worth,
They give it up without a mind
And live their lives in misery and mirth.

Hope is the key that opens doors,
It lets you see beyond the clouds,
It gives you strength to carry on
And never give up, no matter how the crowds.

Hope is a light that shines so bright,
It guides you through the darkest night,
It helps you see the good in life
And never lose your faith in spite.

Hope is a treasure, priceless, yet free,
Embrace its power, let it be.
It carries us onward until the end,
With hope, our hearts eternally mend.

Love, the River of Life

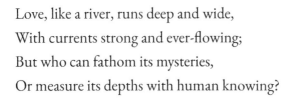

Love, like a river, runs deep and wide,
With currents strong and ever-flowing;
But who can fathom its mysteries,
Or measure its depths with human knowing?

Sometimes it flows with gentle ease,
Reflecting the blue of heaven above;
But then it surges with wild passion,
And sweeps all before its mighty love.

Sometimes it is calm and still and clear,
Like a mirror reflecting the sky;
But then it clouds and darkens with storm,
And its waters are lashed into fury and cry.

But ever and always it flows on,
Through sunshine and shadow, through storm and through calm;
And ever and always it is love,
The great and mighty river of life.

Chapter 14:

The Resilience of the Human Heart

CHAPTER 14: THE RESILIENCE OF THE HUMAN HEART

The Ability to Forgive

To forgive is to set a prisoner free,
And discover the prisoner was you.

To forgive is to let go of the pain,
And realize that the pain was in vain.

To forgive is to open the door,
And let the hatred and anger out.

To forgive is to release the past,
And allow the future to begin at last.

To forgive is to heal the wound,
And let the love flow in again.

To forgive is to be free,
And to know that you are worthy of love.

The Capacity to Love

What is this thing we call love?
A feeling, a state of being?
An emotion, a chemical reaction?
A choice, a decision?

Is it something we are born with?
Or something we learn over time?
Is it something we can control?
Or something that controls us?

Love is a mystery,
A paradox,
A puzzle.

It is the most powerful force in the universe,
And yet it is also the most fragile.

It can bring us great joy,
And it can also bring us great pain.

But through it all,
Love is always there.

It is the one thing that makes life worth living.

The Strength to Endure

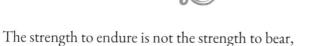

The strength to endure is not the strength to bear,
Nor is it found in stoic calm or pride;
It is the power to rise above despair,
And face the future with a dauntless stride.

It is the power to smile when all is lost,
And find a rainbow in the darkest cloud;
It is the power to hope when hope is most,
And faith when faith is all but drowned.

It is the power to fight when all is vain,
And win when victory seems out of reach;
It is the power to love when love is slain,
And live when life seems but a bitter breach.

It is the power to do, when all is said,
The thing that must be done, no matter what;
It is the power to be, when all is lost,
The best that you can be, for yourself and others.

The Faith to Believe in Yourself

The faith to believe in yourself is more
Than just a feeling, it's a way of life.
It's not about perfection, but embracing your worth,
Trusting in your potential, from which greatness can birth.

It's about knowing that you are capable of great things,
Even if you don't always feel like it.
It's about believing in yourself even when others don't.

It's about having the courage to take risks,
Even when you're afraid of failing.
It's about believing in yourself even when the odds are stacked against you.

The faith to believe in yourself is the most powerful force in the world.
It's the force that can move mountains and change the world.
So never give up on yourself, no matter what.
Believe in yourself, and you can achieve anything.

Tomorrow's Promise

Tomorrow is a day to dream,
To wish and hope that all will be
As bright as one would have it seem,
A day of peace and harmony.

Tomorrow is a day to live,
To love and be loved in return,
To help and comfort those who grieve,
To make the world a better place.

Tomorrow is a day to be,
To simply exist in the moment,
To appreciate all that is good,
To be grateful for each day.

Tomorrow is a day to reflect,
To think about what is important,
To set goals and make a plan,
To live each day as if it were your last.

Seize the Day

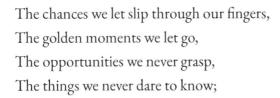

The chances we let slip through our fingers,
The golden moments we let go,
The opportunities we never grasp,
The things we never dare to know;

The things we might have been, had we but tried,
The heights we might have reached, had we but dared,
The joys we might have known, had we but known,
The love we might have won, had we but cared;

These are the things that haunt us ever,
These are the things that make us sad,
These are the things that make us wonder,
If we had only, only had.

Don't let fear hinder, take risks with stride,
Embrace the unknown, let your spirit guide.
Seize each opportunity, make the most of the day,
For in living fully, regrets fade away.

Acknowledgments:

I want to give a big thanks to everyone who helped turn this book from a dream into something real.

To my family and friends, thank you for always being my rock. Your love and faith in me gave me the strength to write this book.

To my dear readers, I sincerely appreciate your time and attention in reading my book and exploring my poems. If they resonated with you, I would be grateful if you could take a moment to leave a review where you purchased the book.

Finally, if you liked my book, come follow me on social media. I share new poems there every day. Every new follower, every like, every share, makes my day.

Instagram: @mosesianpoetry
Tiktok: @mosesianpoetry

Made in United States
Orlando, FL
06 September 2025